Bob Boylan's stuff works. I know because we use it all the time. Buy it, read it and win.
——ROLF PEPPLE, CBS General Manager
WLTE Radio Station

If I could recommend a single book to every manager or leader in the country, that book would be *Get Everyone in Your Boat Rowing in the Same Direction.*
——GREG ALMQUIST, Executive Vice President
Pinnacle Realty Management Company

A vital aspect of leadership is communication. Bob Boylan's approach to effective communication is one of the best in the business. His process works throughout an organization to empower people to be leaders at all levels.
——LINDA MARVIN, President
Lockheed Environmental Systems & Technologies Co.

Bob Boylan's business is effectiveness. Whether he's helping people become better leaders or more productive workers or happier and more balanced human beings, he consistently offers people a hands-on approach to becoming more effective at whatever they want to accomplish.
——BLANTON BELK, President/Founder
Up With People

D0565542

Bob Boylan's approach is so sensible and down-to-earth that much of the time you find yourself slapping your forehead and saying, "Of course! That's exactly what I need to do." And the best part of all is that, when you go do it, it works. This book can help a *manager* become a *leader*!

 —ALAN JOHNSON, President
 Norwest Bank, Wayzata

Bob has helped my organization become better presenters, managers, and individuals. His new book will help us become better leaders ... without tricks, fast talk, or one-size-fits-all explanations. Bob Boylan helps people turn their dreams and goals quickly into solid, positive realities.

 —KEN BANKS, Marketing Director
 Eckerd Drug

My path has crossed Bob Boylan's at three critical stages of my career and the development of my organization. Each encounter resulted in a blast of growth and energy that propelled us fast-forward in our quest for improvement and success. Bob's great new book uncovers the hot buttons of leadership and tells you how to tap into that marvelous energy source—PEOPLE. Highly recommended!

 —RICK GILBERT, Vice President, Regional Manager
 Boise Cascade Canada Ltd.

Get Everyone in Your Boat Rowing in the Same Direction

Get Everyone in Your Boat Rowing in the Same Direction

5 Leadership Principles to Follow
So Others Will Follow You

Bob Boylan

Adams Media Corporation
Holbrook, Massachusetts

Published by Adams Media Corporation
260 Center Street, Holbrook, MA 02343

ISBN: 1-55850-547-4
Printed in Canada.

J I H G F E

Library of Congress Cataloging-in-Publication Data
Boylan, Bob, 1936-
    Get everyone in your boat rowing in the same direction: 5 leadership principles to follow so others will follow you / Bob Boylan.
    p.   cm.
    ISBN 1-55850-547-4 (pb)
    1. Leadership. 2. Employee motivation.   I. Title.
HD57.7.B69   1995   95-41506
658.3'14—dc20   CIP

This publication is designed to provide accurate and authoritative information with regard to the subject matter covered. It is sold with the understanding that the publisher is not engaged in rendering legal, accounting, or other professional advice. If legal advice or other expert assistance is required, the services of a competent professional person should be sought.
    —From a *Declaration of Principles* jointly adopted by a Committee of the American Bar Association and a Committee of Publishers and Associations

This book is available at quantity discounts for bulk purchases.
For information, call 1-800-872-5627 (in Massachusetts, 781-767-8100).

Visit our home page at http://www.adamsmedia.com

DEDICATION

Many people *want* to lead, but few do; they struggle and stumble and nothing much happens.

This book goes to the heart of helping people lead. It tells you what to talk about so that people follow you.

And you end up leading.

I would like to dedicate this book to those people who will actively pursue the challenge of leading others. We need you.

ACKNOWLEDGMENTS

Thanks to my clients who have allowed me to facilitate their Leadership Retreats. The practical knowledge of what is necessary in order to lead has been gained through heated and passionate exchanges at these events.

Thanks to my staff for their professional skills, attention to detail, and encouragement.

Thanks to

- June Gongoll, for making the book come to life through her computer skills
- Geri Sullivan, who formatted the text
- Kathy Oberhauser, for keeping our business running smoothly
- Jack Lindstrom, whose design abilities and business insight brought life, fun, and focus to the end product
- Nancy Miller, whose editing skills kept the multiple rewrites focused on clarity, memorability, and crispness

Thanks to my wife, Judy, whose trust in me never diminishes. Her strong, quiet belief in my insights about leadership truly fortifies my internal strength to tell my story—namely, what I believe it is necessary to talk about and do in order to lead people.

CONTENTS

Principle 1: Decide "What's Important Around Here?"

Principle 2: Ask, "Where Are We Headed?"

Principle 3: Determine Your Credo—"What We Stand For!"

Principle 4: Understand the Need to Fall in Love with Risk

Principle 5: Learn to Motivate People

Conclusion: Now What Do I Do?

THE TROUBLE WITH THE FUTURE IS IT'S NO LONGER LIKE IT USED TO BE

Because of global competition and technology, the future will never be like it used to be. Things simply are more competitive and moving faster. There is always some new technology replacing the one we've just started to get used to.

Much has been written about the crying need for more leaders, visionaries who can point us to a new and better condition, both in our companies and in our world.

This book is for anyone trying to lead, anyone aspiring to lead, and anyone who simply must lead—which includes just about everyone. Every day, you are called upon to lead. The better you do that, and the better you communicate, the more likely you are to reach your goals.

What must you talk about so that people will follow you?

WHAT IS LEADERSHIP?

A few years ago, I made a presentation to the officers who run West Point. I received this opportunity because my cousin, Gen. Peter Boylan, was commandant of the school.

After my day-long seminar on how to communicate more effectively, I found myself sitting in the commandant's home at West Point. The place exuded history. Peter and I talked about what West Point really taught its students.

"Leadership is the key thing we teach and instill in our students," he said.

So I asked him, "Peter, you teach leadership. You are a leader here at West Point. You have been a leader in battle. What is leadership?"

"That's easy, Bob," he said. "Leadership is getting people to follow you!"

I was slightly shocked by his simple answer. "Peter, look at all those books by the fireplace … about all aspects of leadership. There *must* be more to it than that."

"Of course there is, Bob, but the absolute essence is that people have to follow you or, by definition, you are not leading!"

It seemed simple and direct to me. And as my cousin was quick to point out, this definition was not original with him—it is actually attributed to Gen. Dwight D. Eisenhower, former president of the United States. That's good enough for me!

The more I've studied and observed people trying to get things done with, and through, other people, the more I believe this simple definition.

You Don't Lead with Memos

Today's leaders are good on their feet. In fact, they are passionate about "What's important around here?" and "Where are we headed?"

Today's leaders don't just sit in their corner offices and write memos. They are always speaking to their people, up and down the entire organization. They are out and about, practicing managing (leading) by talking to people. *Speaking to people to get them to follow you is what leaders do.*

I'm a consultant to many organizations. I help them discover where they want to go and how they can get there. I've learned a lot about leaders and about leading from people. And I see two essential questions that must be answered by anyone who aspires to lead:

Many books have been written about leadership. Most of them fall into one of two categories: Either they are written by academicians describing the disciplines necessary to lead and the attributes leaders must possess, or they are written by leaders themselves who describe "how I did it at XYZ Company."

All of these books can be valuable. But my professional life focuses on making things happen in organizations, on causing beneficial changes, and on delivering simple, actionable concepts.

So this book will deliver principles and techniques on leadership that are

- Easily understood

- Memorable

- Realistically actionable

Therefore,

- You will have a better chance to put the principles and techniques to use.

- You will have a good chance to reap the benefits of more effective leadership.

What Do Leaders Say and How Do They Say It So that People Follow Them?

All organizations are charged with finding and keeping quality people. Once these people are on board in your organization, they are aching to make a difference—hungry to make a contribution—yearning to be recognized.

You will be successful—you will have people follow you—only when people *think* they are making a difference, *feel* they are contributing, and *know* that their efforts are recognized and their needs ("what's in it for me?") are being met.

To make this happen, you must follow five simple steps, or principles. Once you have done this, your people will know how to act and where they can make a difference. They will also know how they will benefit from their commitment to making a difference.

Leadership is like love. It's something you do, not just think about. It must be *talked* about, not just *thought* about.

WHAT DO LEADERS TALK ABOUT?

Principle 1:   They talk about *what's important around here.*

Principle 2:   They talk about *where are we headed.*

Principle 3:   They talk about *what we stand for.*

Principle 4:   They talk about *falling in love with risk.*

How do leaders talk to get people to follow them?

Principle 5:   They learn to *motivate people.*

These five principles are the essence of what is necessary to lead people. Notice that they all involve speaking—telling and selling your values, your dreams, and why it's so vital that everyone understand how he or she can benefit from working to attain your vision.

This book will take you through each principle and offer practical insights into how to make it all happen.

So that people will follow you.

Principle 1

DECIDE "WHAT'S IMPORTANT AROUND HERE?"

8:30 Is Important Around Here!

One of my clients is a former Marine lieutenant colonel. He's one of these guys who's hooked on being punctual, and to him 8:30 means 8:30. "We start work at 8:30, not 8:35."

He lets prospective employees know this, but sometimes they don't realize how important 8:30 really is.

For example, soon after starting work there, Bill arrived at 8:45 one morning. My client noticed this and asked, "What's up, Bill? You're a little late."

"Well … bad traffic today," Bill answered.

"Plan for that. We start at 8:30."

Three weeks later Bill showed up at 9:30. "My kids were up sick last night. I didn't get much sleep, so I slept in a little longer," he said.

My client didn't respond right away. He had kids too, but his next response was, "Bill, 8:30 is when we all start. Is that clear?"

Five weeks later, Bill showed up at 10:45. As he was busily

going about his work, my client came up to him, fuming mad. "10:45! Don't you remember our previous discussions on the importance of getting to work at 8:30?"

"But, Boss, I stayed late at work last night to finish that hot project you assigned me. I thought you'd understand my coming in later in the morning."

"Well, I don't. 8:30 is what's important here. It doesn't seem like we fit. You just don't understand what's important around here!"

Who hasn't been in this type of situation, where actions can't be explained on a rational basis? Yet situations like this occur because every potential leader has some things that he or she feels are very important. It's the way we *do* things around here, or the way we will *change* and do things differently around here.

These basic values, the answers to the question, "What's important around here?" form the platform from which all leaders operate. They are the foundation on which all directions and plans are built. They are the underlying principles that *will* be lived up to, or you cannot survive in the organization.

What are the "8:30s" in your life?

What personal idiosyncrasies drive your work day?

How do they affect the people you want to have follow you?

"8:30 is what's important around here!"

I Want 10,000 Fireflies over There!

Walt Disney was walking through Disney World, before its completion, with a small group of his department heads. Suddenly he stopped, pointed to a specific area, and said, "I want 10,000 fireflies over there!"

The head of construction asked, "When?"

Notice that the man did not say, "But, Walt, where could I possibly find 10,000 fireflies?" or "Wouldn't 5,000 be sufficient?"

Perfection, absolute top quality, was the value here. Just do it, please. The man said, "When?" No second guessing, just "when?" He understood that for Mr. Disney, perfection was the value—a value the man himself obviously also bought into.

What we have here is a fit between the values of the leader, the followers, and the organization.

In order to have this fit, however, it's important that your potential followers understand your values—what's important to *you*. You need to clearly define this for them. That's the first step.

Then you must discuss the values that are important to *them*. That's the second step.

Finally, together you both need to discover the values that are *actually being demonstrated* in your organization. What makes your place tick? What values have created your corporate culture?

Only after these three ingredients have been discovered and clearly stated can you make the fit with *mutual values*.

DISCOVER YOUR MUTUAL VALUES

In discovering your values—yours and your employees'—begin with the premise that most people have honest, honorable values. They are all good, and neither unethical nor immoral.

> If you are to be a leader, you need to discover your mutual values, the ones you all want to live and feel good about.

One way to do this is to have a professional leadership seminar with a facilitator who can run a "discover our mutual values" session. This session can and should get hot. People are justifiably passionate about what's important to them.

For example, let's take the value of integrity, which I define as doing what you say you'll do. For me, this is the key value in our business, one that seems simple to me. When I'm involved with people who follow this principle (or value), things go smoothly. There are no surprises. Outcomes can be predicted with a fair degree of accuracy.

When I find myself in new relationships with people who do *not* do what they say they will do, I'm exasperated, to say the least.

In fact, I'm mad that these people have violated my trust in them. What is happening here? Our values are not mutually shared.

Here are some values that I've discovered people like to hash out so that they can really define "what's important around here to *all* of us."

- *Integrity*—"Do what you say you'll do."

- *Growth*—"We want to be bigger! Growth is king."

- *Profit*—"At all costs, the bottom line will be good."

- *Professionalism*—"Be the best you can be at your job."

- *Great service*—"Deliver legendary service (so good, it's legendary)."

- *Positive attitudes*—"Grumps don't fit in here."

- *Common enemy*—"We'll do anything to beat the XYZ Company!"

- *Take risks*—"We must try new ideas, even if that means failing many times."

- *Give 110 percent*—"Always. This will not be a sleepy place."

- *Self-management*—"Do what needs to be done without always asking 'Is this OK?' before acting."

- *Quality is king*—"Nothing goes out of our place that's second-rate."

In the space below, list the values that are currently most important to *you* in your job and organization.

1. _____

2. _____

3. _____

4. _____

5. _____

6. _____

Once you've looked at your values as a businessperson, I suggest you look at your personal values. This will balance you out. In the next section you'll discover what *really* makes you tick.

DISCOVER WHAT MAKES YOU TICK

As I was about to turn fifty years old, I found myself at the end of a business trip in Europe. I'd been training *Time* magazine's European sales force, and now I was about to take a six-day vacation alone. It was the first time I'd ever done that.

On a previous visit, my wife and I had discovered a fabulous gasthof in Obermieming, Austria, and I headed to this magnificent spot. Gasthof Schwarz is in a tiny village, surrounded by mountains that allow the spirit to soar.

On a sun-drenched patio, my first morning there, I sipped my coffee after a full breakfast. My thoughts wandered to the fact I would be turning fifty in four months. I almost never think about my age, but "fifty" had a big ring to it.

My life was more than half over. It had been a very, very good life, but I found myself asking, "Why has it been so good? What have I been doing and why?"

So, I started to write

down my thoughts in a very spur-of-the-moment process. What had made me tick for the first fifty years of my life?

I discovered many things. For instance, I realized that we all act out our lives in one way or another. Many times I had not been able to understand why I did what I did, felt what I felt, dreamed what I dreamed. Vague direction can mold a good deal of our lives. It has much of mine.

But the process of discovering what makes us tick awakens personal reflection on the factors in our lives that move us to action, that fuel our dreams. It's a process intended to make you happier, more satisfied with your life.

Discovering the positive elements in my life and how each makes me tick has allowed me to increase the time I spend doing the things I value. The process has worked for me—which is why I think it will do the same for you.

Once you have more clearly defined these values for yourself, you will obviously be able to communicate them better to others. Then you'll be able to surround yourself with people who have the same values.

Below are some values that I've found people often care passionately about.

- *Personal integrity*—Doing what you believe in, care about, and feel is ethical or important

- *Personal growth*—Becoming steadily wiser, more balanced, and more connected with other people

- *Positive attitude*—Looking at what's useful, beneficial, or worthwhile in each situation

- *Self-determination*—Being able to choose what you do and how and when you do it

- *Serenity*—Feeling alert, yet at peace, changing what you can about the world and accepting what you can't

- *Financial security*—Having the money, talents, and/or opportunities to keep yourself and your family free from fiscal difficulties or worries

- *Time*—Spending it with family, friends, personal interests, and/or your own thoughts

- *Joy*—Feeling effective, energized, and a dynamic part of the universe

In the space that follows, list those values that are currently most important to you in all facets of your life. (These don't have to be from the list above.)

1. _____

2. _____

3. _____

4. _____

5. _____

6. _____

Now you really should know what's most important to *you*. But what about the other people in your organization? What makes *them* tick? And, what values does your organization demonstrate, whether you agree with them or not?

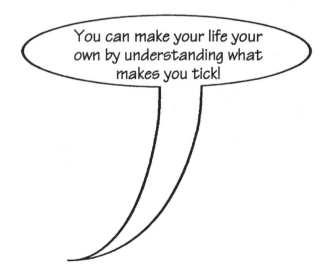

DISCOVER WHAT MAKES OTHERS TICK

In a few pages I'll show you how to take your organization through the process of discovering what's most important to the people in it, and deciding together what values your company will live by in the future. I call this process a Vision Quest, and it can do more for your organization than any number of seminars on motivation, quality, or management theory.

Once, before I began a Vision Quest, my client told me, "Bob, we have two companies here. Even though you see only one company name, we really have two totally different companies."

There are two sets of answers to what's important around here.

As we talked more about this, it became clear to me that there were two different sets of values being acted upon, which in turn created two cultures—i.e., two companies.

This person's arm of the company was focused primarily on providing ever more effective and competitive service to customers. But outside of his division, service scarcely seemed to be a concern. Everyone else seemed to be focused almost entirely on growth and on increasing the bottom-line profit.

This problem exists in many organizations. It can take the form of different sets of answers to the question, "What's important around here?" by department or division or location. Obviously, when that happens, the departments or divisions or locations cannot, by definition, be headed in the same direction. It's impossible. No synergy between departments means the loss of cooperative energy in achieving the goals of the organization.

There can also be two versions of what's important when a company talks about one set of values (sometimes very loudly) but acts on quite another. For instance, an organization may emphasize quality over and over in its advertisements, public relations pieces, and in-house publications. But in its day-to-day operations—the actual business of getting things done—management may, in fact, be far more concerned with high output and low production costs than with quality.

A simple exercise I suggest you do *before* you do a Vision Quest is what I call an Organizational Values Matrix. You do it by yourself first. Later you *may* wish to have your key people do it. Its purpose is to help you define, as well as discover, the values that make different people tick—and those values that are not necessarily yours, but that have become organizational values. Some of them you may like; others you may not agree with at all.

Here's the Exercise

- List your values (what makes you tick—what's important to you) in the left column of the values matrix.

- Write your name and the names of key people in your organization across the top. You can create this matrix by department, division, location, etc.

- On a 1 to 10 scale, 1 being low and 10 high, rank how you see yourself and the other people *demonstrating* in behavior or attitude a belief in that particular value.

VALUES MATRIX FOR YOUR KEY PEOPLE

Discovering What Makes Others Tick

List In This Column What You Believe Should Be Important Around Your Place	Rate Yourself 1–10	Rate Each Listed Person 1–10 (1 is low, 10 is high)		
		Key People		
1.				
2.				
3.				
4.				
5.				
6.				

This values matrix should give you a clear idea of exactly where in your organization there is synergy and where there is conflict. You may be surprised at just how revealing this simple chart can be.

By thinking about other people's values and how they affect one another, you can get a new perspective on how and why things happen as they do. When you look at people's values—the behaviors they follow and the rules they live by—you can more easily see why certain difficulties have arisen and where they have been most likely to arise.

DISCOVER WHAT MAKES YOUR ORGANIZATION TICK

Your next step is to look at your organization as a whole—what behaviors it routinely exhibits and what rules it lives by.

Spend a few minutes thinking about what values your company follows—not necessarily the ones it claims to follow, or the ones you or other people in it follow or feel are important, but the values the organization as a whole acts on and puts into practice day by day.

List the most importance of these values below in descending order of importance. (Refer back to the list of common values on page 18 for ideas if you like, but don't feel limited by them.)

1. _____

2. _____

3. _____

4. _____

5. _____

6. _____

Once you've listed these values, look them over carefully. Do they create a synergy, or are they in conflict with one another? Do they lend themselves to a clear plan and direction, or do they take the organization in several different directions at once?

Now I'd like you to see what kind of fit there is between your company's values and those of the key people in it. To do this, fill in the organizational values matrix on the following page.

- List the organizational values in the left-hand column, in descending order of importance.

- Write your own name and the names of key people in your organization across the top. Once again, you can create this matrix by department, division, location, or any other category you choose.

- On a 1 to 10 scale, 1 being low and 10 high, rank how you see yourself and the other people demonstrating in behavior and attitude a belief in that particular organizational value.

ORGANIZATIONAL VALUES MATRIX

Discovering How You and Others Feel About the Organization's Demonstrated Values

Organization's Values	You	Key People		
1.				
2.				
3.				
4.				
5.				
6.				

It is probable that the three types of values do not neatly fit together. Therefore, in the Vision Quest, you'll need to hash out *what's really important around here?*

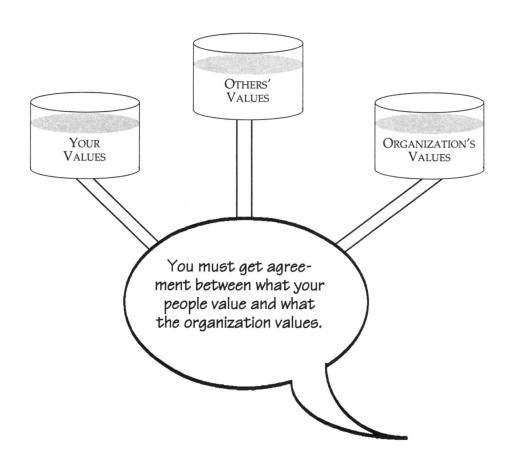

What you have just done is powerfully important. You have defined how you perceive the differences between what's important to *you* and what's important to *others,* and the differences between what's important to the *organization* and what's important to you and to others.

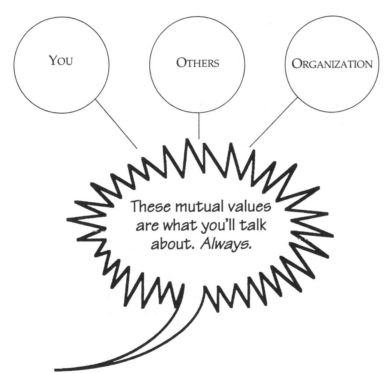

Now the task is to agree on a set of mutual values so that everyone can say, "You bet! That's important to me!"

PEOPLE CAN SOAR OR NOT SOAR

The key to the success of mutual values in an organization is to understand that

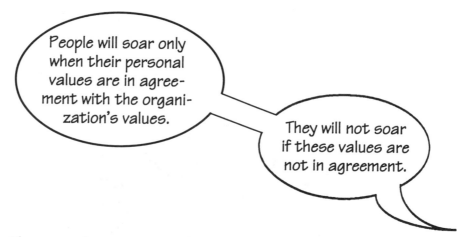

If your values are out of sync with the company's, you are in the wrong place. It's not that the organization's values are wrong and yours are right, or vice versa. It's just that they don't match. And you'll probably need to divorce from each other because not doing so feels bad. Plus, you cannot soar when values are not shared. You just can't.

If you decide to stay, you'll always be disgruntled, irritated, and frustrated. You won't live up to your own potential. And you'll know it.

Two extremely important types of business relationships are those with your employees and your vendors. Here are some suggestions to match up your organization's values with your employees and your vendors.

You can soar!

- During the hiring process, ask a prospective employee to talk about his or her personal values, as well as the values the person is looking for in your organization.

- Give the prospective employee a list of ten to fifteen values any organization might hold. Included in this list will be your organization's values. Ask the person to rank on a 1 to 10 scale the ones he or she feels are really important.

- In the discussion that follows, you and your prospective employee will discover if you both fit—or, better yet, whether the person will soar once employed.

- When entering into a relationship (which you hope will be long-term) with a vendor, it is entirely appropriate to discuss your organizational values and the vendor's. Get these values out in front of you on paper. Look at the key overlapping areas of agreement. See if there are some major areas of disagreement.

After all, you want a long marriage with employees and vendors, not a short-term honeymoon followed by a divorce.

SOME FACTS ABOUT VALUES

Fact: *Values drive organizations.*

- Everything you do is based on the basic values by which you live your life.

Fact: *Values shape*

- Attitudes—how you develop your people

- Policies—how you treat personnel issues

- Procedures—how fast you do things

- Activities—how (if) you really celebrate victories

Fact: *Values are always being demonstrated.*

- You can't hide them.

- You can't claim you have a certain value and then act differently, or you'll be (correctly) labeled a hypocrite.

Fact: *Values create your organization's culture—how the place lives as an entity.*

Fact: *You, as a potential leader, have values. You already know what's important to you.*

- Therefore, you need to clearly state those values to others. You must visualize them. "Make no mistake about it, these are the values that are important to me!"

- Be laser clear. Be brief.

- Then, find out who agrees with you. Those who do will follow you. Those who don't, won't. And shouldn't.

Fact: *Once you get people to agree on a set of mutual values, business objectives will be more easily defined.*

- Organizational direction is based on what you value.

- People will now be easily able to buy in or buy out, to agree or disagree with the direction.

All business objectives are based on values.

WHAT YOU END UP TALKING ABOUT

The groundwork has been laid. The homework has been done. You have discovered

1. What's important to you

2. What's important to your people

3. What the organization has been demonstrating is important

4. Agreement on your *mutual* values, the values you are "collectively passionate" about

> Leaders need to continue to drive home the organization's shared values every time they speak.

> When people can identify what they are passionate about in terms of what the culture is going to be like so that they can thrive in it, you'll have a group of people who can now tackle the question *"Where are we headed?"*

When a leader can constantly talk about values that everyone has agreed to, there is a "buy-in" by the followers. They know that the organization's fundamental principles are in keeping with their own values. Since there will be a sense of ownership when these shared values are talked about, people will tend to come to decisions faster and define objectives more easily.

It's like an emotional and psychological goose every time you hear the leader talk about the shared mutual values of the organization.

You say to yourself,

"Those are my values, too. Let's tackle that problem!"

So—What's Important Around Here?

CHAPTER CHECKLIST

- ✔ Discover what makes you tick. What's important to you? What are *your* values?

- ✔ Discover the values of those whom you wish to lead.

- ✔ Discover the organization's values.

- ✔ Discover your mutual values. Realize that it's smart to have shared values.

- ✔ Get agreement on what's important around here.

- ✔ All business objectives are based on values.

- ✔ The strength of an organization is the strength of the shared values within it.

- ✔ Leaders must continue to drive home the organization's shared values every time they speak.

Principle 2

ASK, "WHERE ARE WE HEADED?"

THE NORMAL SITUATION

In most organizations, few employees can answer the question, "Where are we headed?"

In fact, a recent Booz, Allen & Hamilton study revealed that only 37 percent of senior officials think other key managers clearly understand business goals.

Well, that's not so good. However, it's normal.

How does this happen? Because no clear direction has been established by the leader.

Or if one has been established, it hasn't been communicated forcefully, or memorably, enough for people to know where they are headed.

A leader without a vision—a direction in which he or she wants to take the organization—is simply not a leader.

A leader without a vision has no rallying cry. Therefore, inconsistent messages are uttered every time the person opens his or her mouth. No one really can answer with any clarity or conviction the big question: "Where is our organization headed?"

THE SECRET TO CREATING A VISION

> The secret to creating a vision is first having defined your shared values.

Once organizations absorb the obvious wisdom of defining shared values *first*, then the next logical question to be answered by the leader is, "Where are we headed with all these people who want to work together?"

Too often, however, the question "Where are we headed?" is asked too soon. There is almost no discussion, at least in a formal sort of way, of the key question that I believe comes first: "What's important around here?"

At a recent Vision Quest I was conducting, I asked all the key players a simple question: "How big do you want to be in dollar volume in three years?" And I added, "OK, tell me your current annual sales so that we can have a benchmark for where we'll be moving from."

To my astonishment, of the thirteen people in front of me, only four knew the current annual sales. Two of these were the owners, so really only two others knew where they were now—let alone where they wanted to go. (By the way, these thirteen people were the key department heads of a 128-person company.)

The two owners were flabbergasted. They also quickly learned that their communication to the troops of what's up lately had been sorely lacking.

Once we got the current annual sales established, we moved on to "What do you want that number to be three years from now?"

Everyone thought. Some took out calculators. Some looked puzzled, as if they had no control over the issue to begin with.

Then I went around the room, got everyone's forecast, and put the numbers on a flip chart. Everyone was amazed. The range was from essentially no growth over three years to slightly more than doubling in size over those same three years. Some valued aggressive growth as essential, while others saw it as downright stupid.

People were either elated or scared because what was important to them was being challenged by asking "how fast should we grow?" when starting to define "where are we headed?"

I've played out this example more than 100 times in the last fourteen years as I've conducted Vision Quests for organizations.

> The key to answering "Where are we headed?" lies in *first* answering "What's important around here?"

If you choose to violate this principle, you'll define a vision that will not be supported by everyone. And some people will work actively to sabotage your vision, because *it is not based on what is important to them.*

WHAT'S A VISION?

A leader needs to possess a spark of genius—the ability to assemble from a wide variety of inputs and historical data a clearly articulated vision of the future. This vision needs to be

- Simple

- Easily understood

- Clearly desirable by all

- Energizing

Warren Bennis describes a vision as a condition that is better in some important ways than what now exists.

John Nesbitt, in *Reinventing the Corporation,* calls vision the link between dream and action.

A vision has a wholeness about it. It is not just a sales forecast. "We're going to reach $350 million in sales in five years! Isn't that exciting?" is not a vision.

But a vision must also be realistic and salable to the team.

Some time ago, I had as a client a company whose president had a vision of growth that far outstripped what anyone imagined could be achieved. It simply seemed totally unrealistic. In addition, the president made the initial mistake of trying to force people to believe it. When that obviously was not working, we held a Values and Vision Quest. His key people redefined an *achievable* vision based on their mutual values—and because they believed in it, it *became* achievable.

Lee Iacocca is an outstanding example of someone who created a vision of success that mobilized large factions of employees to align behind it. He empowered them.

So we can see that a vision is the second step to leadership. Without it, there is no focus. A good vision grabs. Its passion helps transform purpose—where you want to be—into action almost automatically.

A strong vision is compelling. It pulls people toward it. It commits people to action and converts followers into leaders.

Vision gives an organization a glimpse of its collective potential. It gives meaning to why you belong to an organization. It answers the question, "Where are we going?" It defines direction.

No one has expressed vision more clearly than Fred Smith, CEO of Federal Express, in the book *Absolutely, Positively Overnight!* That's a crystal-clear vision. A stake in the ground. A rallying point.

To summarize,

A vision is a condition that is better in some important ways than what now exists.

A vision:

- Grabs

- Focuses

- Arouses passion

- Transforms purpose into action

- Compels

- Pulls people toward it

- Commits people to action

- Drives a stake in the ground

- Says "That's what we'll be!"

- Becomes a rallying point

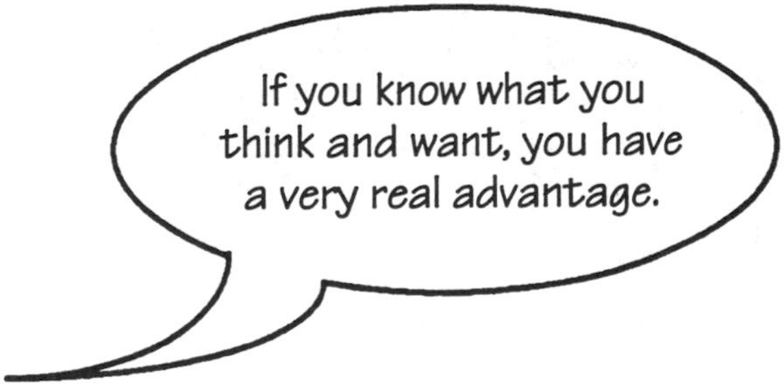

If you know what you think and want, you have a very real advantage.

But this is still nothing to get too excited about. A vision created solely by the boss is hard to sell to the troops. Therefore, you need to create a *mutual* vision. Without it, you'll be all alone with your grand vision; no one will own it but you. And no one will really help you get there.

WE HAVE NO MUTUAL VISION!

About five years ago I was holding a Presentation Skills Workshop for Gardner Advertising, a large national advertising agency in St. Louis. The agency's top eight people were at the session.

One specific presentation exercise was to answer the question, "Why am I hanging around Gardner Advertising?" (The purpose was to allow each presenter to present from the heart.)

The first two presenters did a good job talking about the people they loved to work with, the creative challenges, etc.

Then a bomb was dropped!

The third presenter (who happened to be the senior client services person in the agency) said, "The reason I'm hanging around is because we *used* to be good. We're not good now. We still have great people, but we have no mutual vision! I'm hanging around in case we define our mutual vision because it would be so exciting being good again."

Each of the next four presenters echoed the exact same thoughts, all using the term *mutual vision.*

But they never did define their mutual vision. The president never wanted to take the time to discover what was really important to his people and in what direction they wanted to be headed. He was always too busy handling the current business.

It's sad, but since this company never decided where it was headed, based on shared values, today it is literally out of business. The doors are closed. Hundreds of people are out of work.

It's the leader's responsibility to define what that something is.

BENEFITS OF A MUTUAL VISION

The most compelling reason for a crystal-clear mutual vision is that it gives all the people in the organization a point on which to focus their skills and brain power. It gives them the chance to be as good as they think they are.

A mutual vision allows for self-motivation.

The keys to developing a mutual vision are to understand that

- You cannot mandate the vision or impose it on potential followers.

- Like any other product, your vision is something you must sell.

It does no good to go to the mountaintop and dream up your vision all alone. If you do, you'll find you're also all alone in buying into it and trying to make it happen.

You simply cannot mandate your vision and have others help you get there.

Therefore,

The first question an aspiring leader must answer is, "What do my people want?"

You need to begin with what you want *and* what your key people want and need. And you'll have to understand that the only reason any of us do anything is "What's in it for me?" (WIIFM). Your potential followers have WIIFM on the brain.

So

Don't sell a vision, sell the *benefits* of the vision.

John Nesbitt lists a number of benefits people will discover in defining their mutual vision:

- A strong vision can link a person's job with that person's purpose in life.

- The office will not be a sleepy place.

- People will achieve goals more easily.

- People will experience ownership of the vision; therefore, they will really know what they should or could be doing and why.

- Day-to-day activities will make things really happen.

- Growth will be focused, and therefore easier.

- There will be a good balance of work and fun.

- An organization's vision will free people to manage themselves.

The key to having happy campers working in your organization is giving your people the chance to grow, both personally and professionally. People beg to make a difference with their lives and add a meaningful contribution.

A mutual vision that states where you are headed gives your people the responsibility for getting the organization to where you want it to be. Once a vision is accepted, the responsibility for attaining it is shared. In other words, you're not going it alone as a leader.

For Bill Gore, the founder of Gore-Tex, "Commitment to a vision, not to authority, is what produces results!" Leaders want results, so allow your people to create a mutual vision to which they can become committed.

A mutual vision gives people a chance to be as good as they think they are.

A leader who creates a vision that is meaningful to followers, and benefit-oriented to *them*, will find people who will be self-motivated to attain the vision—*their* vision.

And once the mutual vision is accepted, everyone shares the responsibility for attaining it.

How Do You Create a Mutual Vision?

One way to create a mutual vision is to have a Vision Quest. As the leader, you select a place away from your office or normal place of business. Then schedule a day with all your key players, so that no one is missing. The day must be labeled as "very important."

A few weeks before the Vision Quest, hold a brief meeting at which you will define the purpose of the Vision Quest, set up the day's schedule, and plan the follow-up activities. You might start off the meeting saying something like this.

> It's finally dawned on me that maybe not everyone knows where we as an organization are trying to go. You know, what road we're trying to follow, what path we're taking—what we really are striving for.
>
> As your leader, it's my responsibility to help define that direction for you. That's part of my job description. As they say, it goes with the territory.
>
> However, I can't get there alone. I need all of you to help share where you think we should go. What do you see out there through your own eyes? What would you like this place to become?
>
> Therefore, I've scheduled a day for all of us to explore what we are to become. What's your vision for our organization? What exciting, yet realistic, picture do you see for us in the next three or five years? [I've discovered that people have difficulty getting excited about anything further away than five years.]

With these questions in mind, I'd like each one of you to prepare your thoughts on how you see us three years from now with
regard to these areas:

Our gross income
Our net income
Number of employees
Amount of office/manufacturing space
Location of offices/plants
Market share
What our success will be based on
What we will be known for
What position we will occupy in our industry (market)
Why people will want to work here

We will have an outside facilitator guiding us through the
process of discovering where we are going in each of these areas.
Maybe other parameters will surface while we discuss our vision.

I realize I'm responsible for setting the final vision, for defining the dream that will benefit all of us.

But I need your input. I have to be sure that the vision we shape
for this organization is one we are all excited about and one that we
all will share responsibility for. *We need to define our mutual vision.*

This Vision Quest is vital to our company. We're going to
decide where we're going. Be ready to do just that.

That's the kick-off meeting.

Now reserve a good place—one that's well ventilated and well
lit, and that has plenty of wall surface to pin or tape up flip-chart
pages as you facilitate the process.

Next, select an experienced facilitator. Find someone who understands the process and its value, and who can get people to contribute in a focused manner. It's also important to have a facilitator who can add knowledge and ideas to the process.

Then, when the retreat is over, you must return to your office with all the valuable input, and distill and define your organization's vision. As former President Harry Truman so aptly stated, "The buck stops here!"

You are the one who decides. You must write a crystal-clear vision that will be beneficial to the majority of your key people—a vision they have already convinced you *they* are excited about, and, obviously, one *you* are excited about.

Warren Bennis proposes a couple of ways to choose what your vision will be:

1. Your vision should create enthusiastic commitment because it is

   - Right for the times
   - Right for the organization
   - Right for the people

2. A crystal-clear vision

   - Feels right
   - Appeals to the gut
   - Resonates with the listener's own emotional needs
   - Somehow clicks

I agree with Warren Bennis when he says,

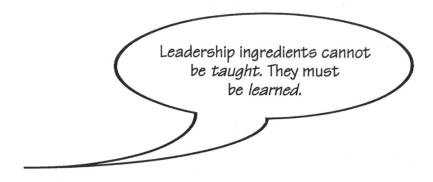

Leadership ingredients cannot be taught. They must be learned.

One way you learn is by really listening to your people as you go through the process of creating and defining your mutual values and mutual vision.

People are willing to follow if they are sold on believing that following is in *their* best interest.

Once you have a clear organizational vision, I suggest you meet again with your key players. Present it to them. Sell it to them. Motivate them to buy into it.

Your vision is intangible by itself. You must use emotional benefits to get the buy-in—emotional benefits that make the vision tangible.

ONE MORE TIME: WHY HAVE A MUTUAL VISION, ANYWAY?

The whole reason for creating a vision can best be summarized in this story.

To give meaning to why you belong to an organization.

Two stonecutters were chipping square blocks out of granite. A visitor to the quarry asked what they were doing.

The first stonecutter, looking rather sour, grumbled, "I'm cutting this damned stone into a block."

The second, who looked pleased with his work, replied proudly, "I'm on this team that's building a cathedral."

A worker who can envision the whole cathedral and who has been given responsibility for constructing a portion of it will be far more satisfied and productive than a worker who sees only the granite.

A true leader is one who designs the cathedral and then shares the vision that inspires others to build it.

So—Where Are We Headed?

CHAPTER CHECKLIST

✔ Fact: Most people cannot clearly state where their organization is headed.

✔ The key to answering "Where are we headed?" lies in *first* answering "What's important around here?"

✔ A vision is important.

✔ A *mutual* vision is the only way to go so that

  ✔ People have a chance to be as good as they think they are.

  ✔ People become self-motivated.

✔ Once a mutual vision is accepted, everyone shares the responsibility for attaining it.

✔ This fact allows you to have a very good chance of arriving at your vision. Really.

✔ People are willing to follow if they are sold on believing that following is in *their* best interest.

Principle 3

DETERMINE YOUR CREDO— "WHAT WE STAND FOR!"

EVERY LEADER NEEDS A CREDO

Every day you will be talking to people inside and outside your organization. These people need to easily and clearly understand where your firm stands relative to similar firms with which you compete.

The listener needs to be able to position your company as a certain kind of company, offering a product or service with certain benefits for people with certain needs.

Now that you have figured out your mutual values and mutual vision, creating a strategy (a plan) to get to where you want to go is a must. Obviously.

The key part of the strategy to get to where you want to go is your answer to "Who are we, anyway?" stated in a crystal-clear sentence or phrase.

Who are we, anyway?

This statement is your credo, your position. It needs to clearly differentiate you from others selling similar products or services. It needs to be benefit-oriented, and it needs to address a particular target audience.

This credo is what you actually talk about. It is your external rallying cry. It is what you'll say every time you get up to speak. It will be what your company's capabilities presentation is based on.

It's you.

It's what you live for.

It's why you exist.

It's what will give you sparkle when you speak.

It's what your people must buy into, so that you can deliver it.

It's what you believe.

It's what everyone in your organization must believe.

Always.

THE DIFFERENCE BETWEEN VISION AND POSITION

Leaders need to talk about where they're headed. That's your *vision*.

Leaders need to talk about what they stand for, what they deliver, who they are. That's your *position*.

A vision is where you are going.

A position is who you are, your identity.

In the reality of business, position is more important than vision. A credo is the short line that is the essence of the position. It's what gets talked about to *everybody*, inside and outside your organization.

Your credo will institutionalize your vision and make it a reality.

Your credo allows you to be remembered and differentiated.

Your vision is essentially an *internal* issue. The financial analysts want to know it, as does your banker, but mostly it's used only inside, to give direction to activities and to let your people know the goal—where you are headed. You have to have it in order to create a mutual buy-in so that everyone knows where the team is heading and why it's beneficial to get on the bus!

Your position is largely an *external* message. It allows your public to know what you do, what you stand for, what's different about your product or service, what's the benefit of your product or service, and who you want to do business with.

The whole idea of knowing who you are and what you stand for is so simple, yet also so profound and sophisticated. It's difficult to pull off, but without it there's no chance to institutionalize the vision and make it long-term and lasting.

Your credo is the essence of your position, your "line."

You *must* have a credo!

"WE'RE THE BUSINESSMAN'S AIRLINE"

I experienced a beautiful example of a crystal-clear position a few years ago when I was doing business in Oslo, Norway, and took a weekend ski trip to a resort six hours north of the city to see some of the beautiful countryside. Speaking to a young Norwegian couple on Saturday night, I asked the young woman, "Who do you work for?"

She responded, "SAS" (Scandinavian Airlines).

"What do you do?" I asked.

"I'm a reservationist."

Then I posed a very simple request: "Tell me about SAS."

"SAS? We're the Businessman's Airline," she said confidently.

Somewhat startled by her crisp response, I listened as she added in an even more self-assured tone, "We want everyone to know that we're the Businessman's Airline."

Now that's a crystal-clear position.

Jan Carlzun, president of SAS, had a vision, "to become the best airline in the world for the frequent business traveler."

In his book *Moments of Truth*, Carlzun states that in order to attain his vision, he and his people decided to position themselves as the Businessman's Airline. This position gave Carlzun a credo by which to measure all decisions. He talked about it to all of his people internally—and, of course, his advertising and sales messages focused on why SAS was *the* Businessman's Airline.

In fact, since that experience in Norway, when a young woman who was a reservationist for SAS clearly sounded off with the company credo ("We're the Businessman's Airline"), I've also checked with many other SAS employees when I fly their airline. Would you believe it, *everyone* knows this. In fact, SAS employees get heated and excited when they tell me the benefits for a businessperson of flying SAS. They're sold. And they sold me. (By the way, it also helped move SAS from a company on the verge of losing $20 million in 1981 to one that just one year later was earning $54 million. By 1984, SAS was voted *Air Transport World*'s Airline of the Year.)

If your organization has a credo now, and you're out talking about it with consistency, then your people will "test" as well as the SAS people. But if you don't have a credo, a consistent message to talk about, your people don't know what you stand for.

CONCENTRATION IS THE SECRET

Positioning is essentially a marketing concept created to help companies differentiate their products in the consumer's mind. For example, if you sell tires, how do your tires differ, to the customer's benefit, from other companies' tires?

This still is a vital rationale for positioning—to clearly differentiate.

However, I believe there is another equally valid rationale for positioning: the *principle of concentration.*

Take the SAS position, "We're the Businessman's Airline." This position allowed (or forced) all planning, capital investments, advertising, training, etc., to be measured against one concentrated target.

The target, "to become the world's best airline for the frequent business traveler"—in other words, "to be the Businessman's Airline"—provided a clear, concentrated focus so that SAS could (and did) attain its vision.

The business principle of concentration can be looked at like this:

Concentrating your resources gives you a fighting chance to attain your vision.

Down the road, your board of directors, or your boss, or someone, will ask you, "Well, did you ever get to where you said you wanted to go?"

Genuine fear can engulf you when you envision that question. But fear is a legitimate motivator. Since you want to say, "Of course we are on track," or "We hit the target," I urge you to create a position so clear that it allows you to concentrate your resources.

The principle of concentration seems simple, yet it eludes many organizations. So many of us try to do a little bit of everything, try to please so many audiences—and never become great at anything.

Management by committee fosters this type of thinking, an example of which is giving an equal amount of resources to each operating division. This seems "fair," but it isn't—because, by definition, not all divisions have the same opportunities to get a good return on invested capital.

When you see this type of equal distribution of resources, you know that the firm does not understand the principle of concentration.

The leader's role is to clearly point out the direction of the organization, then position the organization so that there is a credo to live by.

A leader must demand loyalty to the vision and credo.

Then everyone knows that's what you stand for. Therefore, that's what your resources must be concentrated toward, so that you have a fighting chance to deliver against your credo.

This sequence of activity will automatically create a strong identity for your organization.

ORGANIZATIONAL IDENTITY CREATES ORGANIZATIONAL INTEGRITY

When you have high integrity, people trust you to do what you say you'll do. Without trust, not much happens smoothly. Trust is the emotional glue that binds an organization together.

And trust generates more integrity.

Integrity requires consistency, and consistency requires focus and concentration. Without focus and concentration, it's almost impossible for your company to be consistently good at everything it does. With focus, however, there is the realistic hope that it can be very good at the few things it concentrates on and becomes known for. It's these few things that will differentiate your company from others.

That's the heart of positioning. That's *why* you want to have a crystal-clear position, a crystal-clear credo that the you talk about.

An organization can create high integrity by having a high degree of organizational identity.

Identity Yields Integrity

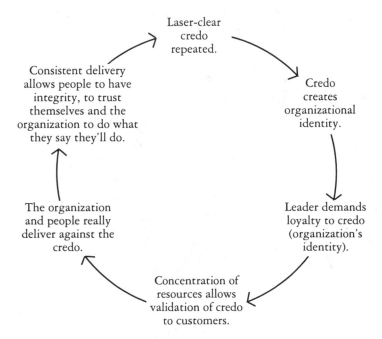

When leaders burn in the company credo by continually talking about it internally and externally, organizational identity is created.

When people repeatedly hear the credo—who we'll be to get to where we are headed—they learn to believe it. The leader demands loyalty to the position, to the company credo.

And when the position flows from mutual values and a mutual vision, demanding loyalty to it should be a piece of cake.

Now everyone can concentrate on delivering services and products that fulfill the position. Resources are also concentrated. Where this occurs repeatedly, customers realize that the organization and its people are demonstrating integrity. They really deliver what they say they will.

Trust is generated in these people themselves when they know that they actually do consistently deliver against the credo. They really trust themselves and the organization to do what they say they will.

Now people feel confident and have pride in the place. They walk around saying the credo with gusto! Now lots of people repeat the credo. They believe.

Why? Because they "own" the credo; it is their credo. By fulfilling it, the mutual vision will be reached, and they know they will benefit from that.

It all starts with a laser-clear credo that the leader continually talks about.

THE THIRTY-SECOND ELEVATOR RIDE TEST

If you have a laser-clear credo that you and your people talk about, you can pass this test.

If you don't, you'll fail it. And lots of other opportunities to tell your story succinctly.

Here's the Thirty-Second Elevator Ride Test.

Imagine getting on an elevator for a ride to your office on the thirty-second floor. Sharing the elevator with you is just one other person, someone you've nodded to hundreds of times, but never talked to.

After a comment about the weather and morning traffic, this person says, "You know, I see you many times every week, but I've never known anything about your company. Tell me about your place."

You have about thirty seconds before you get off the elevator. In this amount of time, can you clearly state:

1. The name of your company (not too tough).

2. What you stand for/believe in (very tough).

3. The benefits of your product/service (tough).

Try writing the answers to these simple questions now, for your company. Just 2 and 3.

2. _____

   _____

   _____

3. _____

   _____

   _____

Most people cannot answer these questions in thirty seconds. This means the leadership has not addressed who your company is (your credo) and how that benefits your customers.

Every day, hundreds of opportunities present themselves to people at all levels in an organization. Theoretically, people at *every* level should be able to state the company credo and explain how it is translated into benefits to the customers. You never know when you may be talking to a potential or current customer who needs a boost to the rationale for doing business with you.

Everyone needs to be able to talk about these core issues:

1. Who are we? How do we differentiate ourselves from companies delivering similar products or services? This is your credo, your position.

2. How does our credo benefit our customers?

A leader who constantly talks about the credo will discover that almost everyone can recite it. A leader who doesn't is missing the mark, losing the chance to turn the entire company into a sales force with a basic selling message:

1. The credo

2. The benefits to the customer

Try this thirty-second test on your employees to discover how clear you've been in communicating your own credo. Even if you know you don't have a clear credo, find out what your employees say . . . because they'll say something. It may be far off the mark, but it's their perception of reality—and to them, that's the truth.

You have the right to expect everyone to know your credo and to be loyal to it—once you've done the work to make it laser-clear.

Your people will love the feeling they get when they can pass the thirty-second test. It will reinforce why they work for the organization. It will give them a boost—plus, now they will be able to convincingly talk about who you are.

CREATE CAMP CREDO

In order to discover who you want to be to get to where you're headed, you need to attend Camp Credo.

Camp Credo is an off-site two-day retreat for all the key players in your organization. You go to Camp Credo *only* after

- You have defined your mutual values.

- You have defined your mutual vision.

You create Camp Credo because you simply will no longer tolerate the verbal mishmash you currently spew out when asked to explain your organization. You realize that you need a credo so that you have a *line* that embodies who you are, a line that you will talk about.

You must have a credo
to talk about.

It is at this point in the process of leading that many organizations become unglued. Deciding "what we do best, for whom, and how" can become tangled with so many hidden agendas and people protecting their own organizational turf that the entire process can collapse in disarray.

Invariably, organizations discover that they don't agree on what they're good at, what they want to keep doing, what they want to stop doing, who they want to work for, and what kind of clients they'd rather not work for. It's tough to agree.

But if you want to lead,
you must have a credo.

Therefore, what is essential *before* Camp Credo convenes is a clear understanding of the outcome of the camp. *"We will decide on a credo. Period."* This is the battle cry before you go to camp because you must have a credo to talk about or you will not be able to lead the troops—or be memorable to your customers.

To attend Camp Credo, the key players must prepare to discuss or present the following information in accordance with this suggested agenda:

Agenda

1. Visualize the key values your organization has decided to embrace. Make sure these values are clearly understandable to everyone and that agreement is reached on the following:

   - What drives us

   - What makes us tick

   - Whether you can say, "Yes, that's us" or "No, that's not us"

   - What people must understand about:

     - Working for us

     - Buying from us

     - Selling to us

How will you clarify these values for *all* to know so that they permeate everything you do?

2. Visualize the key points of the mutual vision, in terms of

   • Dollar growth.

   • People growth.

   • Facilities growth.

   • New products/services.

   • Definition of customers/prospects.

   • Mix of business changes. What are the major segments of your business that create income? Will the percentage that each segment delivers change from the current mix?

   • Changes in market share.

   • Major competitors.

3. List the major indicators of performance you measure to see how your organization is doing. These might include growth rate, product line depth, price, service, quality, distribution, technology, etc.

4. List all competitors.

5. Create a matrix comparing your organization with its competitors. Rank each company against a major indicator of performance over the next three to five years. Use a 1 to 10 scale, with 1 being poor, 10 being very good, and 5 being average.

6. Discover how the picture will look after three to five years. See what changes will probably occur. One simple, yet amazingly effective way to forecast how you and your competitors will grow over the next three years is to determine your average annual growth rate and that of each competitor (you'll need four years of statistics to create a three-year average compound growth rate). For example, a 15 percent compounded growth rate per year will double the size of a company in five years. Then you simply project each company's growth over the next three years at its historical growth rate. The rationale? Most organizations tend to grow in the future at the same rate they have in the past.

7. Research any changes that could have a major effect on your industry—changes that might be brought about by
   • Government regulation or deregulation

   • Environmental concerns

   • Census changes

   • New technology

   • Closely aligned industries (e.g., what personal computers did to dedicated word processing machines)

   • Competitors changing their marketing strategy, their mix of products, their distribution systems, etc.

8. Estimate the likelihood that any of these external changes will happen and, if they do, how they will change the picture you have painted of how the marketplace will probably look in three years.

   Don't get too bogged down in this process or you'll never recover. It may seem like you are playing God, projecting all the things that will happen. But use your combined industry and market sensitivity, your own chutzpah, to project the likelihood of any of these changes happening to your organization three years down the road.

9. Now summarize where you are. You should have a fairly good picture of how you see your organization in relation to your competition. You've also gone to the top of the mountain and looked at possible external changes and how they would affect the picture. Reach a consensus on how the market will look. You may wish to develop two or three different scenarios based on external changes.

10. Now discuss the following questions:

    • What do we think our organization does best?

    • What do we think our *customers* think we do best?

    • What do we think we do that benefits our customers the most?

    • What do we do that truly differentiates us from the competition and benefits our customers the most?

- What else do we do that truly differentiates our organization from the competition for our employees and our stockholders?

Cover the walls with flip-chart paper so that the answers to these questions confront everyone.

Don't forget, if you really do not know what your customers perceive to be your strong suit, find out through good research. After all, you want to continue to sell what your customers have clearly defined as your major strength and what is most beneficial to them. Only your customers really know you. Find out what they think and believe.

At this point, you might want to tell the story about the catering managers of a large hotel chain who met to discuss their professional opinions about what makes a good coffee break for people who hold meetings in their hotels.

The answer they all agreed upon was

- Outstanding-quality coffee

- Beautiful chinaware

- A beautifully packaged coffee service table

Then one of the younger catering managers said, "I'm new here, but why don't we ask the people who take the coffee breaks, our customers, what they think makes a good coffee break?" So they did.

Imagine their surprise at finding that their customers' idea of a good coffee break was:

- Fast service

- Coffee close to the telephones

- Coffee close to the bathrooms

Notice that they never said

- Good-quality coffee

- Beautiful chinaware

- A beautifully packaged coffee service table

Know what your customers want!

THE VIEW FROM A HELICOPTER

The next to last step Camp Credo employs relates to Ken Blanchard's concept of "Get a helicopter view of your situation by hovering over it."

My experience as a facilitator at many of these retreats is that joining metaphorical thinking with the helicopter view is a fascinating and fun exercise.

Metaphorical thinking helps us understand the unfamiliar by means of the similarities it has with what *is* familiar. This kind of thinking gives us a different slant on the problem. In using metaphorical thinking combined with a view from a helicopter, you get an overview of your company with a twist—a twist that will have truth. A twist that will be clear and clean. A twist that will bring you closer to your credo.

To do this, simply ask everyone at the session to review all the information on the flip-chart sheets on the walls as if they were hovering over the entire meeting in a helicopter.

You can say, "It's necessary to start to summarize everything and decide just who we are, what makes us different, and how that benefits our customers. What's your bird's-eye view of everything that's being said?"

Let them review and make notes for fifteen minutes. Then hit them with this: "And here is a little surprise. Now I want you to take five minutes and write the answer to this request: 'Please explain our company in terms of a fruit.'"

Continue, "Be honest. You'll get to the truth quickly. Be positive, but also point out areas where we're not so strong.

"Creativity is fostered best in a spirit of laughter. I expect to hear some giggles, even while you are writing. Then in five minutes we'll go around the room and everyone will read what he or she wrote.

"Expect to discover truth—who we really are, and how quickly metaphorical thinking will free us to explain it."

I've worked for many organizations as a consultant. This exercise *always* produces fresh insight, and focuses people on the strengths and uniquenesses in their organizations.

One such experience was with the Up With People organization. This thirty-year-old organization has touched millions of people in more than twenty-five countries with its message of "People are good everywhere." But explaining Up With People is quite difficult, for it is different things to different groups: one thing to its cast members, something else to its sponsors.

By way of background, Up With People is an organization that offers a one-year experiential education program to about 600 college-age students from twenty-five countries each year. The students learn a musical show, and travel and perform for eleven months, while living with host families in over 100 different cities, both in America and abroad.

My assignment was to help the organization explain to its prospective sponsors, "What is Up With People?"

While working with the sales force, I posed this situation:

"Put yourself in the shoes of a typical sponsor, for example, a vice president of marketing for a bank. As the bank's marketing person, you have decided to buy a four-day Up With People package for your town. Now the cast has come to town, done their thing, and left.

The sales force all looked puzzled and then began writing. In five minutes, time was up.

So I asked, "Who has something?"

A twenty-eight-year-old woman stood up and said, "Speaking

as the vice president of marketing for a bank who just had the cast come to town—well, Up With People is like a shiny red apple.

"You see, eight months ago, when Susan came to our bank and introduced the concept of sponsoring an Up With People cast for four days, she played a videotape showing all the places the cast had performed. I saw all those bright faces and all that energy. It reminded me of a bushel of bright shiny red apples. So we bought a four-day sponsorship.

"Then your cast came to town, and our bank employees housed them. We bit into those apples and discovered that they all tasted a little different. Different backgrounds, cultures, races, interests, etc. Just as each apple tastes different.

"Yet when the cast performed at our local hospital, nursing homes, and even a school for the deaf, we discovered that the 'core' of Up With People was the same: People caring about one another, caring about common values, all wanting a better, more peaceful world.

"Then the cast put on its two-hour musical show and we all saw live, on stage, 130 shiny red apples. Such electricity. Such energy!

"As the cast left town, they left the seeds of the apple so that we could keep growing the spirit of people touching people in a variety of community involvement programs."

The other salespeople sat with their collective mouths open, somewhat awestruck. I said, "I don't know about you, but if I were selling Up With People next week, I'd walk into a prospective sponsor's office, take out an apple from my briefcase and say, 'Mr. Prospect, let me tell you why Up With People is like a shiny red apple.'"

Metaphorical thinking allows people to discover truth, both good and bad. It allows them to express themselves in memorable ways. It's a great exercise to clear away the cobwebs in the brain so that we can discover who we are and create our position—our credo of who we want to be to get to where we want to go.

Metaphorical thinking helps you figure out what you will talk about.

THE MAGIC BILLBOARD

I've facilitated many Camp Credos (I used to call them positioning retreats), and I've learned that the single best exercise to help people discover and then decide on who they'll be—their credo—is something I call the Magic Billboard Exercise.

This is the final exercise in Camp Credo.

The Magic Billboard Exercise forces each person to use the best computer in the world, the brain, and fosters use of both the logical and the creative sides of the brain. Each participant must define the essence of what he or she wants to say—in effect, how to describe the credo for the organization.

A credo is a strong, crisp, clean statement of what you believe in, what you stand for.

Here's how you run the Magic Billboard Exercise:

1. All the flip-chart paper you've used in Camp Credo is taped up around the room so that the visual impressions of the two days of discussions can bombard the brain.

2. Everyone is given one hour to write a billboard that explains your company—your credo—on a flip chart. It must be written using the rules for good outdoor billboards:

   A. Use six to eight words.

   B. Use a visual that can make it even clearer, if possible.

3. Each person outlines the rationale that supports his or her credo.

   A. Why is it the best way to say who you are so that you can become who you want to be and arrive at your already-agreed-upon vision?

   B. Why will this credo drive you to deliver strong benefits to your customers? What will those benefits be?

   C. How does this credo stir the emotions of your people internally?

   D. What disciplines will need to be improved (or will automatically improve) when this credo becomes your main belief? What will become your battle cry?

   E. Why does your credo:

- Seem right for the times?

- Appeal to the gut?

- Seem to be a realistic stretch toward what you will strive to become, while still being supportable with current evidence? (Don't forget, you have to be able to say something tomorrow, not just what you'll be in three years.)

4. *Now here comes the magic!* Each person stands up and presents his or her billboard with as much commitment as possible. Each person gives supporting evidence, answering the issues in Point 3 of this outline.

   • Everyone receives applause at the end of a presentation. It's high-energy time. All ideas are valid. No negative comments are allowed.

   • Expect magic. Don't be afraid to get excited.

5. *Don't forget, you've decided to decide!* You decided that the outcome would be a definite credo. It's very possible that you'll hit it on the spot. Magic can happen. For sure, you'll agree on the essence of the credo, and someone will then go and write it for final approval.

6. *Allow immediate magic to happen* (even if the exact words need to be fine-tuned). All the participants will feel a sense of ownership. Their thumbprints are on the credo. Therefore, they own it and will be committed to supporting it.

Now you will have a very good chance of reaching your vision!

America's Leading Glass Fabricator

When the eight top people of Viracon, a division of Apogee Enterprises, Inc., started out at Camp Credo, none of them realized what a huge discovery they were about to make.

All were experienced in glass manufacturing and were marketing professionals. The company was growing substantially each year and making good money. Jim Martineau, the president of this division, had also been its founder some years earlier. He'd built a good team. Things were healthy.

Jim and the team were also disciplined and knowledgeable about their industry. After completing all the informational matrixes, we got down to what really differentiated Viracon from its competitors.

This may seem strange, but the team discovered (meaning that they didn't know it when they walked into the room) that Viracon was the leading glass fabricator in America! That's right, number one! The leader!

Once the team uncovered who Viracon was, the leader, they immediately could see some strategies they could create and execute to take advantage of their leadership role in their industry.

Their credo, "Viracon Is America's Leading Glass Fabricator," became the platform for measuring internal quality control, distribution, product development, marketing programs, etc.

The sales force stood taller. The company's capability presentation was more focused and exciting.

The leader and his people now had something to talk about. And are they having a good time talking about it!

Step-by-Step Planning

Grand Forks, North Dakota, is not America's hotbed of advertising agencies. However, Simmons Advertising has been in business there for over forty years and is a strong, well-regarded regional agency.

Fred Lukens, president of Simmons Advertising, used my services to help clean up an already existing new business growth plan. The agency was healthy and moving along quite well. It had an extraordinary number of very bright, well-educated people and experienced advertising professionals.

After spending the entire day defining the agency's strengths, weaknesses, and goals, I sent all the participants home to create their magic billboards. They were told to present their ideas on flip charts first thing the next morning.

After a couple of people presented their billboards, Joy, the media director, got up. And magic happened!

She said, "You know, we all think we're good planners, but why we're so good at it is, we always plan step by step."

She continued, "We always do things in order, not out of sequence. We never let things fall through the cracks or eliminate or shortcut a step in the process out of expediency. Never. We always do our planning *step by step!*"

She was passionate and evangelistic. She sold all her own peers and her boss. Fred was really excited.

So I suggested that we find something that has steps. A stepladder was produced to help visualize steps.

We discovered that it had seven steps. Simmons's current planning process had fourteen steps. "Why not make it a seven-step process?" someone shouted (really shouted). "It's too long now, too confusing for everybody."

Another person said, "Yeah, let's engrave each of our seven steps on a brass plate and affix the plates to a real step-ladder and put it in the lobby. A memorable symbol."

The credo was born!

Step-by-Step Planning—
Simmons Advertising.

Today Fred has a custom-made, oversized solid oak stepladder in the lobby. And yes, every step has an engraved plate calling out a specific planning discipline that Simmons follows.

Fred, by the way, is 6'8" tall. Guess who actually climbs up the ladder, with a client or prospect climbing up the other side, during a pitch? Why? To symbolize that both client and agency are solidly grounded on a broad platform of information. And both are striving for the same objectives at the top. (As you know, the stepladder is broader at the bottom and comes together at the top. Great symbolism!)

Simmons has stepladder pins, a desktop-model stepladder, and a newsletter called *Step-by-Step Planning*.

Do you think Fred and all the people there know what to talk about when they explain who Simmons is and how it differentiates itself?

Of course. In spades!

And what do you think shows up at the prospect's home after the pitch, before the decision? Guess.

What's your credo? What's your visual symbol? Try to top Fred's story. After all, Simmons is only in Grand Forks, North Dakota.

So—Who Will We Be?

CHAPTER CHECKLIST

✔ Until you have a credo, you don't have a core idea to talk about. There's no rallying cry, no clear-cut cause to repeat to motivate internally, and to explain and position your organization externally.

✔ Don't confuse your *vision* with your *position*. Your vision is your direction, where you're headed. Your position is what you stand for and deliver. It's your identity. Without your position, you will not institutionalize your vision.

✔ A laser-clear credo will give focused direction, so that with relative ease you'll know where to concentrate your physical, financial, and human resources. However, without a solid concentration of resources, the credo does not live, does not become real. Then all you have is a nice theme line with no substance. No reality. No commitment to the credo.

✔ When you consistently talk about the credo, you will develop, over a period of time, a clear organizational identity—and, with constant repetition, integrity; people will trust your people and what they promise to deliver.

✔ Camp Credo is where the work takes place. It's high energy and an incredible team-building exercise. The key is to decide *before you go* that you will decide on a credo as the outcome. The outcome will not be more meetings, or they'll go on forever.

✔ Your credo is the essence of who you have decided to become so that you will get to where you are headed.

✔ Visualize your credo everywhere you can. When people open up their personal computers each morning, there it is: the credo and its major benefits to your customers.

Your credo is the single most important idea you will constantly talk about.

Principle 4

UNDERSTAND THE NEED TO FALL IN LOVE WITH RISK

FALLING IN LOVE WITH RISK

> At the heart of the visionary is the essence of risk.

Risk is the ingredient that gives adventure to my life and wakes me up. Adventure and risk go together. Risk in my life gives me a chance to claim victory. And victory means celebration. No risks taken, and it's just another day at the office with expected results.

Through risk, we gain a perspective on what it means to be alive, to try new things, to challenge, to accept the possibility of failure as well as success. In my experience,

> I've found few leaders who want to be a slave to certainty.

Leaders find it easy to risk because their commitment to the vision is so strong, and so clear to them. It's already theirs. That's why they sometimes don't even see the specific tactic or strategy as risky.

When you've created mutual values as your foundation for defining your mutual vision and position, you'll discover that everyone will be willing to take risks to attain this mutual vision. In fact, things won't seem very risky.

In the final analysis, when a leader ventures out on the road to the promised land, with a vision and a solid, well-thought-out strategy, the risks are so well defined that the entire team almost forgets that part of the strategy was based on some risky assumptions or projections. When everything runs as planned, they look on the leader as a visionary. When things don't go well, they call the leader a foolish risk taker.

The essence of risk
lies at the heart
of every leader.

WEBSTER SAYS RISK IS A NEGATIVE CONCEPT

There's some real irony in Webster's definition of risk, which explains it in negative terms only:

> **Risk:** the chance of injury, damage, or loss; dangerous chance; hazard. in insurance, a) the chance of loss, b) the degree of probability of loss, the amount of possible loss to the insuring company, the risk of insuring, taking a chance.

Amazing. All downers. No wonder most people look at risk with downright fear. We've been taught to, even by Webster.

This is why I believe it's mandatory for a leader to weigh not only the hazards but the opportunities afforded by risk. What's on the other side of hazard or loss? Seems like there's got to be good news: gains, successes, contributions, victories.

Unfortunately, those who do not learn to love risk close the door to leadership. The potential negative outcome simply seems too large a hurdle to tackle. And it doesn't help when most employees nod their collective heads and say, "It's too risky. We'd better stay where we are.

A leader weighs the opportunities afforded by risk.

We know the waters too well to venture into unknown territory. Let's stay put."

Leaders have to understand the nature of risk. They have to look at all sides of the issue, the positives and the negatives. Then they'll have a better chance of convincing potential followers why they should risk.

AN IDEA THAT ISN'T RISKY IS HARDLY WORTH CALLING AN IDEA

Almost everyone agrees, with gusto, that things are more competitive than they used to be. You bet they are.

This fact creates the necessity for new ideas to be not just a little off center, but *substantially* different. Really different, so that there is a new, clear, competitive difference, a reason to do business with you.

Therefore, by definition, ideas in today's business climate have to be risky in order to cause change that is substantive.

If you propose ideas that cause only minimal change in direction, policy, service, etc. . . . well, the troops would probably have found those without you. They don't really need your leadership to make the change. They'd stumble into the minor changes by themselves.

Leaders need to be on the cutting edge, with risky ideas that can march their people into new ways of doing things.

WHY RISK?

Change is a necessity for staying alive, for being current, and for growing healthy.

Change is today's byword. Like it or not, the world is changing faster than ever. If you want to "stay on it," you need to change with it.

However, everyone knows that "change is good for everyone but me." So attitude is all-powerful when you want to make something happen.

> I see two major reasons to risk:
> • To change.
> • It's stimulating.

You're going to need a lot of ammunition to answer the question, "Why change?"—which, I believe, is the same question as "Why risk?" Risk necessitates change, and most people, most of the time, directly relate change to risk. They want things to stay as they are.

Since you are strongly suggesting a new vision and a new strategy for getting there, obviously some changes are going to have to take place.

Ergo, risks must be taken to cause change.

Change/risk taking is the cornerstone of all leadership. Leaders thrive on it, emotionally and logically.

John Akers, IBM's former chair, has said, "We change our organizational structure every five years just to change. It keeps the troops fresh. Nothing gets stale."

Peter Drucker, in one of his earliest books, *Managing for Results*, feels, "If you're still doing the same thing five years from now, it will be outmoded by competition. You'll be outpaced."

Mark Twain believed, "Loyalty to petrified opinion must be broken." A leader's job is to do just that: break the logjam of petrified opinion.

Why Risk?	Because your commitment to the vision is burning within you.
Why Risk?	Because it is stimulating to think, act, and live that way.
Why Risk?	Because unless you are willing to take risks, you will suffer paralyzing inhibitions.

Why Risk?   Because if you don't, you will never do what
                 you are capable of doing.

Too many people do what they're supposed to do, *not* what they want to do, because the risk seems unbearable.

In fact, my experience with organizations has proven without a shadow of a doubt that

How to Make Risk Less Risky —and More Fun

Risks are taken in the context of a correct set of balanced values, when the vision and value statements of an organization are prepared *by* and *for* its key players. Therefore, you take risks that are considered by all to be in *their* best interests, to reach *their* vision, not just yours. Now you have some wise risks being taken. And the risks seem less risky.

This concept goes to the heart of empowering others to risk. A leader empowers people, pulls rather than pushes, attracts and energizes people to a vision of the future. A leader motivates by identification with the vision, by aligning followers with it, not by rewards or punishment. Everyone is given the green light to take risks in order to attain the vision because everyone is so committed to the success of the quest.

My theory is to *reward* risk, not just tell people to risk. Set up some system that reinforces trying, risking, and failing. Tom Watson of IBM said,

> If you want to succeed, double your failure rate.

Put another way,

> If you haven't failed,
> you haven't tried
> very hard.

It's a constant process—trying, risking, winning some, losing some. That's the game.

> A second reason
> leaders risk is
> because it's
> stimulating.

All of us will be the same five years from now with the exception of

- The books we read
- The people we meet
- The places we go
- The risks we take

Leaders want to be different five years down the road.

Leaders view life as driving—sometimes in forward gear, sometimes in reverse (although not intentionally), but never in neutral.

Every fresh idea I encounter, each new person I meet or place I travel, each risk I take makes me feel more alive.

Leaders celebrate victories and learn from defeats. How dull life would be without celebrations—and without some experiential, forced learning, the kind our mothers were talking about when they said, "This is good for you."

Swinging from the heels gave Reggie Jackson an illustrious, highly paid career in baseball. Mr. October risked big. He also struck out a lot.

Most leaders are attackers, not defenders.

Attacking is stimulating and requires tons of homework and due diligence. You sweat. You're on the offensive. "The best defense is a good offense."

Leaders can never get too excited about just playing defense. It's boring and produces no great press clippings in the trade press.

Brook Knapp said, "There are two kinds of people: those who are paralyzed by fear, and those who are afraid . . . but go ahead anyway."

The great Karl Walenda, the famous tightrope walker, said, "Being on the tightrope is living. Everything else is just waiting."

SHE FINALLY STOOD UP TO SPEAK

Learning to be a better presenter involves risk. The reasons are obvious and visible. You're at the plate, and you'll do *something,* between hitting a grand slam and striking out with the bases loaded.

I teach, "If you want to be a better presenter, you will need to do some things that are physically different from what you are currently doing."

Here's a beautiful story involving physical change, and an obvious risk a woman took in disregarding the cultural practice inside her banking organization.

I was training a group of senior managers at a large Midwestern bank. One of the women said that she could not maintain good control of her audience while presenting. Also, she did not feel that her message was delivered with much authority.

I asked, "What do you do?"

"Well, I sit in the middle of our conference table with about twelve people and go through my presentation."

I said, "Why don't you stand up and use a variety of visual aids to add more impact to your presentation?"

She looked at me with astonishment, as if I had said a naughty word. "Well . . . you don't understand. At our bank we don't stand up in these meetings!"

I added a number of additional ways in which standing up would solve her control and authority problem, but she interrupted me. "I said, we don't stand at our bank!"

One month later I received a critique of an actual presentation she had given. She said she had used some of my ideas to gain control and improve authority. She had also stood up to give the presentation. Her boss told her afterwards, "That's the best presentation I've ever seen in this room!"

So it was a big day in her life. Plus, she showed others how to do something different to make a difference.

THE KEY TO HAPPINESS

While writing *Passages*, her extraordinarily popular book on the stages of adult life, author Gail Sheehy came across an incredibly lucky group of people. She called them "people of high well-being," and they made her intensely curious. "How," she asked, "had they achieved such a state of fulfillment and happiness?"

Sheehy was really asking the question: "What is the key to happiness?"

Sheehy's happy people were beautiful and homely, very bright and only so-so, and set for life or spending more than they could save. In fact, they were far more different than alike. But Sheehy ultimately discovered that these happy people had seven things in common.

One of the seven things these happy people shared was this: *They all had taken a very significant risk in their lives.* Faced with a choice between taking a safe walk and scaling Everest, they had chosen ice axes and heavy jackets.

Some had fallen. Some had fallen, got back up to climb, and fallen again, over and over. But all had tried. And from that, all had been rewarded.

"It is only by risking that we really live at all," someone once wrote, and the evidence for that is all around us.

> They all had taken a very significant risk in their lives.

In reading Sheehy's thorough evidence, you will become convinced that not only is taking risks necessary for leadership and business,

Taking risks is necessary
for your soul.

I've personally discovered the following:

- Overcoming a little danger in my life builds confidence. For example, downhill skiing always makes me risk.

- Through risk, I gain perspective on what it means to be alive, to try new things, to challenge, to accept the possibility of failure as well as success.

- When I risk, there are victories and there are defeats. Celebrations follow victories. Learning follows defeats.

- Risk gives adventure to my life. It's not a sleepy existence. Risk wakes me up!

- The ability to risk is a quality to model, to pass on to my family, as well as to those with whom I work.

WHY FLIRTING WITH FAILURE ALMOST ALWAYS GETS SUCCESS'S ATTENTION

"Always do what you are afraid to do."
—EMERSON

It's easy to see why so many risks work.

Americans love underdogs; it's a fundamental American trait. So when you take a risk in this country, thousands of people root for you, and many end up helping you. In short, the mere fact that your risk *is* a risk enhances your chance of succeeding.

A risk also is unexpected. So it catches your competition unprepared.

Just as likely, a vision with a risk energizes your people. They see in your vision both great rewards if they succeed and heavy penalties if they fail. Choosing a risky vision, then, puts both a stick and a carrot to work for you.

A risky vision also is more likely to energize your people because it is new. As every advertiser knows, *new* is one of the most appealing words in our language. A new vision appeals to a basic human need for novelty. It confirms that life is not, as the author of the famous bumper sticker suggested, "just one damn thing after another."

Imagine the reverse: a safe vision. What makes a vision safe? The fact that it's been attempted before and succeeded? But the fact that something has been done before is evidence that it will not succeed again, because, in marketing terms, that niche already has been filled!

There may be nothing more risky, then, than a venture into the known.

To borrow again from the wisdom of great advertisers, the legendary Bill Bernbach said: "Safe advertising is the riskiest advertising of all."

Safe visions are risky, too

RISKING YOURSELF: YOU'RE NOBODY UNTIL SOMEBODY HATES YOU

Over a once-rich-with-promise company in Minneapolis presides Jay Wilson,* an executive who lives to be liked. To his potential followers, he appears to be consistently cordial, flattering, and positive.

Naturally, these people initially think that Jay is very nice. But they eventually decide otherwise. They realize that Jay is usually *not* nice to his people. He just wants them to *think* he is wonderful.

Eventually, everyone catches on to Jay's act, and many people end up hating him for it. As a result, lacking the benefits that come from honest leadership and respectful criticism, his company has stalled.

Jay has failed to realize that the nicest thing you can be with people isn't nice. It's honest. People don't want dubious praise and feigned support. They want to know where they stand, how they're doing, and the future they have with their company.

I've dubbed this "not-really-that-nice-after-all" leadership style the Gerald Ford syndrome. Of all recent American presidents, none had more "friends" than Ford. None said as many nice things to as many people. None earned as many invitations to pro-am golf tournaments.

---

* I have changed this person's name to protect his anonymity.

What Ford's apparent niceness didn't earn him, however, was true followers. Almost everyone liked Ford, but virtually no one was willing to vote for him in 1976. Ford was not a leader.

Don't communicate nicely. Communicate honestly, tactfully, and respectfully, in a way that earns your people's permanent respect instead of their temporary affection.

Communicating openly and honestly may seem like a risk. It certainly feels like a risk. But it's a risk every leader must take. Vince Lombardi didn't win three Super Bowls by congratulating his linebackers on missed tackles.

How Do You Risk?

First, you get committed.

Then it's easy. Everyone following you will share the vision and values of the orga- nization. Everyone will embrace risk as part of the design of the strategy.

As a leader, it's an absolute necessity that you demand loyalty to the vision and strategy. Obviously, it's not always possible to *demand* that someone share your organization's values.

When you have clearly defined the vision, values, and strategy captured in your company credo, people who are not in agreement will leave on their own. If they don't leave and they con- tinue to torpedo your efforts, then you should show them the door.

You risk by not having total agreement on where you're going and the basic road you intend to travel to get there. Without agree- ment with the vision, no one will accept even the smallest of risks, even the slightest change from current practice.

With agreement, risk taking is a natural course of action, a nec- essary course by definition.

So how do you risk?

First, you get agreement on your values and vision. Then you go outside the square.

One of the oldest puzzles that teaches how to look at problems in a different light is the one below.

Connect all nine dots with four straight lines while never taking your pencil off the paper.

People usually can't do it. What they do often looks like this:

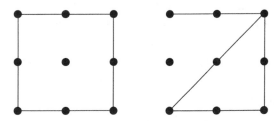

Notice that they never go outside the imaginary lines of the square created by the nine dots. They simply stay inside the normal parameters of thought in attempting to solve the problem. They don't venture out into new territory. They don't risk. Ergo, the problem can't be solved.

The solution to the nine-dot problem? Go outside the imaginary lines of the square.

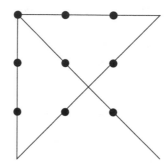

When I was thirty, I had a mentor who taught me this way of thinking. He said, "Bob, for the rest of your life, from this point on, every time you have a problem that's large enough to require alternative solutions, make sure one of the alternatives is outside the square before you select the best one. Make sure one of the alternatives stretches your mind. It may not be the best idea, or the one you'll choose, but I want to look inside your head at least once a month and see how many stretch marks are on your brain."

He meant it. And so do I. This principle is the single best guiding light to test whether you are really taking risks. *Always* make sure that a good share of your alternatives are outside the square. By the law of averages, some of those risky ideas will be good and worth trying. And you're risking—doing things outside the normal way of looking at the situation.

When you go outside the lines, it's scary. It's lonely. It's risky. It's new territory.

This poem, "Coloring," by Sarah Maney, further explains what I'm talking about.

COLORING

Coloring
outside the lines
is scary business.
Some days
I don't have the courage
for it
at all.

On my big, bold days,
though,
I let my red crayon
just streak across a line.
Then I swirl
my purple and orange
out there with it,
in perfect freedom,
no lines.

Coloring
outside the lines
is lonely, too.

I'm the only one
who doesn't get
a gold star
on my paper.
The teacher frowns,
the kids
call me weird
or dumb
or retarded.

Why don't they see
that I'm not behind them?
I'm out in front,
running free
outside the lines.
It would be nice
to have a friend
who colored outside the lines
sometimes
too.
Would you?

Several years ago, Mike Vance, who speaks on creativity, said that an engineer in a session he was facilitating attacked the nine-dot puzzle with zeal. He solved it, then said, "Mr. Vance, if I solved problem A by selecting the solution that was outside the square, the next time problem A comes up again, wouldn't I have to go further outside the lines?"

Vance said, "You got it!"

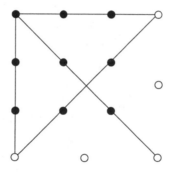

You can see that the square is now bigger and that you must go out even further to risk again.

During the many Camp Credos I've facilitated, there has been a consistent discovery: Most organizations do not seem to have any *systems* for generating ideas—ideas inside as well as outside the square.

Too many businesspeople do not think of themselves as creative. We are all born with the gift of creativity, but we seem to be taught not to use it by phrases like:

> "It's too radical."
> "That's contrary to policy."
> "It won't work in our industry."
> "Can you guarantee that it will work?"
> "It worries our lawyers."
> "It would be impractical."
> "We could never market that."
> "We don't have the time."
> —From ROGER VON OECH
> *A Whack on the Side of the Head*

The main issue to be addressed when linking creativity to risk is this: *You can learn to be more creative.* Learn to come up with more ideas to help develop your strategies. Many brainstorming techniques can be systematically used to help generate more options and insight. More alternatives usually help lower the risk level.

I believe that applied creativity will be one of the main techniques of the future. It will allow companies to make major advances toward their aggressive visions because they will have a disciplined approach to being systematically creative. Reducing risk by creating more options to select from is one form of "doing the right things, not just doing things right."

At the very heart of every visionary is the essence of risk. Being able to see the future as better and somehow different itself carries with it the ability to risk.

One of the most touching things that has ever happened to me involves the nine-dot square.

My client in this story was again Up With People.

One of the sessions I hold with cast members focuses on goal setting and its importance in showing each cast member how he or she is responsible for maximizing their year with Up With People.

During the session, I facilitate the cast members' writing of two types of goals:

- Realistic goals (inside the square)

- Risk or "stretch" goals (outside the square)

Realistic goals need to be touchable, to have a good chance of happening. Risk goals are created only by going outside the square. I show the cast members the nine-dot square and explain the concept of going outside the square to risk. These goals are truly "stretch" goals, the kind you have to sweat a little to reach. As Leo Burnett, a legend in the advertising world, said, "Reach for the stars and you won't come up with a handful of mud!" (By the way, you should see their eyes light up when they start to write their stretch goals. They get excited about going outside the square to risk, to be better than expected, to really push for some growth.)

The experience that truly touched me happened in May 1988, when I was working in Oslo, Norway. I had discovered an Up With People cast performing in Copenhagen, at Tivoli Gardens. It was the same cast I had spoken to about goal setting in November 1987, and so I flew to Copenhagen to surprise the cast and see them perform.

When I arrived and the surprise was over, one of the cast members came up to me and said, "Mr. Boylan, I want to tell you how you have literally changed my approach to living. It's the most significant thing I've ever been taught. And you taught it to me."

"What is it?" I responded.

"Let me show you," she said.

She opened her purse, took out a pen, turned her back to me, and seemed to be writing. When she turned around, she held up the palm of her left hand. On it she had drawn this with a felt-tipped pen:

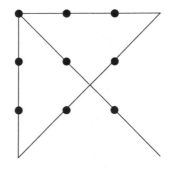

Thanks

We both started to cry. By the way, that's the real pay a consultant receives: making a difference in a person's life.

How do we risk? We get committed, take a long shot, and go outside the square.

So—Why Risk?

CHAPTER CHECKLIST

✔ Risk is the core of leadership. Without embracing it, without falling in love with it, you simply will never voice your vision. You'll keep it inside.

✔ You need to be responsible for accepting risk as the only way you'll ever make a substantive move toward reaching your vision of a better condition.

✔ Risk puts pizazz in your life. Risk gives it zest, zing, vitality. It's the reason you can celebrate victories. If there's no real risk, there's no real celebration.

✔ People accept risk in order to change. Change is synonymous with risk. Change is mandatory to improve conditions, to get to your vision of the future.

✔ You accept risk for two reasons:

✔ Your commitment to your vision is so intense that you'll move mountains to reach it. You'll do what hasn't been done before in your quest to reach the vision. You'll persevere.

✔ Risk is stimulating. It keeps you fresh, provocative, ahead of the pack, leading. It just seems to be part of what makes you up. It's actually fun.

✔ The only way you will risk is to get committed to a vision. If you're not really committed, you'll find that the strategies to reach the vision will be lukewarm, not risky, not big enough to probably ever get to the vision. Change requires risk. An old Chinese proverb says, "It's very difficult to leap a large chasm in two bounds."

Principle 5

**LEARN TO
MOTIVATE
PEOPLE**

You've Got to Be Able to Motivate People

"How you attract and motivate people determines your success as a leader."
— RICHARD SCHUBERT,
    Red Cross Director

You can follow the first four steps and still fail.

For over half of my professional life, I've been teaching middle and senior managers of corporations how to improve their presentation skills, how to be better on their feet. Remember,

You can't lead with memos.

There's a wide difference between a person's *competence* and *effectiveness,* based on that person's ability to communicate verbally.

We are not paid just for our competence. We are paid to be effective. And this effectiveness is usually measured by

- Our productivity

- Our ability to get people to follow us (so that more people are working on the right things)

The sad reality is that there are some bright folks who have followed the first four ideas we've talked about, but still can't get anybody to follow them because they can't motivate people to act. To move. To "do it!"

The bad news is that there are a lot of folks in this spot. Either they don't have the skills to motivate, or fear stops them from getting on their feet and saying, "Here's where we should go. Let's go!"

So nothing much happens. Frustration reigns. Nothing changes. There are no visible defeats from trying—and no celebration of victory.

The good news is that these skills can be learned. They are not inbred, or available only to those few who have been touched by God.

Once you've created a mutual set of values and a mutual vision that allows for self-motivation, your motivational skills don't have to be evangelistic in quality.

Warren Bennis says, "Leaders have no interest in *proving* them-selves, but they have an abiding interest in expressing themselves."

To be successful in moti-vating others, you'll need skills to be able to express yourself.

WHAT ARE WE SELLING?

To begin with, a *leader cannot mandate a vision or impose it on potential followers.*

> Like any other product, your vision is something you must sell.

You cannot assume that everyone will just buy in to your vision and position, even when they've been created jointly. You need to lead people. Get them to follow you by talking about the four areas we've previously discussed.

Potential followers have WIIFM tattooed across their foreheads.

The only thing they are really interested in is the answer to the question, "What's in it for me?"

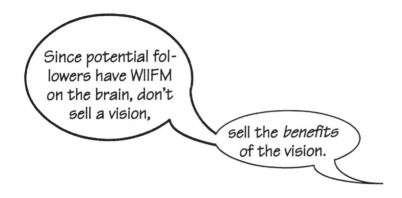

Too often, the leader spouts off about "how big we're going be in three years. We'll be the leading brand if we accelerate our growth. We'll have a new plant if we hit our sales targets, etc."

And the people reply, "That's nice . . . but so what? What's in it for me?"

Don't assume that growth, more plants, more people, and a better market share are automatically thought of as good things.

The savvy leader learns the skills needed to be an effective motivator, an effective presenter, an effective salesperson.

One of the keys is to understand that *your vision is intangible by itself.* You must use emotional benefits to get the buy-in.

Benefits come in two forms: logical and emotional. Emotional benefits are much more powerful.

Logical Benefits	*Emotional Benefits*
• Money	• Recognition
• Time	• Security
• Productivity	• Pleasure
• Efficiency	• Achievement
• Safety	

Leaders work with *emotional* resources. Therefore, you'll need to learn to talk about emotional benefits in order to tap the emotional resources in your organization.

Then, once you have defined the emotional benefits of your vision to all your troops, the vision will become tangible. By the way, the emotional resources of your people are the most powerful resources any organization has!

It's so clear:

Emotional benefits will make the vision tangible.

People are willing to follow if they are made to believe that following is in their best interest.

THE ONLY WAY TO MOTIVATE

Without a carefully constructed vision that will benefit all, it's basically impossible to motivate people to act. They don't have a clear picture of "What's in it for me?"

Therefore, if your vision is ill-conceived and felt to be yours alone, you have only two ways to motivate: fear and intimidation. You can order people to act.

This is the process that is acted out in many companies every day, in places that are not fun to work in. People there don't try very hard to excel or to be as productive as they possibly can be because they don't have any understanding of where they're headed; there's no vision that's exciting to them.

So you've got a glum bunch of people, and every day you have to motivate them to "get more done, faster, with better quality, because

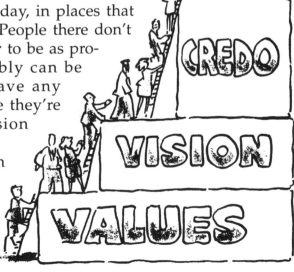

if you don't . . . ," and so the story goes. That's leadership by *pushing*, not pulling.

The best way to motivate is to get people to act toward something in which they have a vested interest. No vested interest, no motivation.

Leadership by pulling requires building long-term trust in

- Where your organization is going

- What it will be and stand for in order to get there

- The values or ground rules by which everyone must play

When these three ingredients of leadership are clearly defined for all to understand and benefit from, then and only then have you created the climate to motivate people to act, to accept risk, and to change. You are able to pull them with you, so that they're now following.

For your vision to become reality, it must be their vision, too.

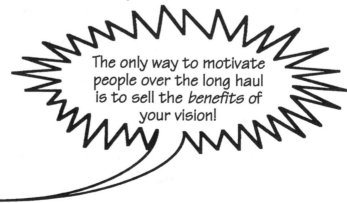

WHY MOTIVATE?

As you can see, you have to motivate people to help get you where you want to go, to realize your vision of the future.

> So that others help you get to where you want to go.

Today's business world talks about empowering people to act. With the proper climate, it's possible to empower people to act, since they see themselves as acting on their own behalf.

You motivate to create momentum. There is a concept of the mass required to make a difference. Once you attain a certain mass, things seem to happen. But that mass doesn't just happen. A leader motivates and orchestrates proposed activity.

Leaders are paid to

- Set the direction.

- Establish the plan.

- Motivate the troops to join the team.

- Shoot to reach the goal.

In fact, the bottom-line task of a leader is to motivate others to follow. If no one follows, nothing happens. The bottom line is to get them to act.

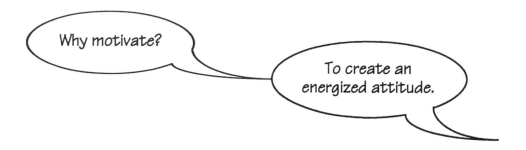

Clayton Barbeau, a counseling psychologist from San Francisco, says there are basically two kinds of folks:

1. Energy givers

2. Energy suckers

He believes we all fall into one category or the other. I believe him. My own experience in getting people to follow me forces me to be an energy giver. I can never get people to follow me when I'm glum, bitter, angry, or tired. They don't raise their hands and say, "Sure, I'll go along with you." Why should they? I don't look like I've bought the idea myself.

When we think of motivators, people like Zig Ziglar and other well-known professional speakers come to mind. They are called "motivational speakers," and people pay good money to hear them. This must mean that we think we *can* be motivated if only the right person, with the right message, tells us what to do.

I'm a professional speaker, and when I tell people that, many times they immediately ask, "Oh, are you one of those motivational guys?"

I've always said, "I hope so, not just to get people hyped up, but to get them to go do something they have a vested interest in!"

In summary,

What's motivation? Getting people excited so that they act in a focused direction.

You are trying to move people in a *specific direction*, not just move them so that they feel better.

You've Got to Be Able to Tell Your Story!

Read what Jan Carlzun, CEO of SAS, says in his book, *Moments of Truth*, about taking on the responsibility to motivate—and the value he places on communicating effectively:

- We couldn't order our employees to do things differently. Instead, we had to convey our vision of the company and convince them that they could and should take responsibility for carrying out that vision.

- *A good leader spends more time communicating than doing anything else* . . . communicating with employees to keep them all working toward the same goals, and . . . with his customers to keep them abreast of the company's new activities and services.

- From my first day at SAS, I've made communicating with our employees a top priority . . . half of my working hours.

- You must consider the words that the receiver can best absorb and make them your own . . . there is no such thing as an "oversimplified" phrase.

- After a speech people often tell me, "That was a phenomenal way of getting across obvious points." I'm not always certain whether they mean it as a compliment; maybe they're not certain either. But I believe I have successfully conveyed my message if what I said has come across as obvious. It means I have found a way to express something that strikes a resonant chord inside the people who are listening to me. I have reached them.

- There is no question that the kind of leadership communication I am calling for involves more than a little showmanship. If you want to be an effective leader, you cannot be shy or reticent. Knowing how to appear before large audiences and persuade them to "buy" your message is a crucial attribute of leadership, almost as crucial as being able to calculate or plan.

- Unless you can communicate your business strategy clearly to your customers, you might as well not have developed it at all.

Ever hear someone complain, "He was just too darn clear?" Of course not.

> Your goal is to persuade people, not to show them you know more than they do.

Leaders must tell a laser-clear story. Repeatedly.

Pretty heavy stuff. No communication skills—no actualization of the plan. Why have a vision at all if you can't get people to follow you?

IF YOU'RE EXCITED, NOTIFY YOUR FACE!

Telling your story clearly is one thing. Telling it so that it looks as if you've bought into it yourself is another.

How many times, when witnessing someone giving a presentation about something he or she *says* is important, have we seen the person start off well, but in a few minutes revert to the predictable, monotone, flat-faced, dull-sounding company line.

If it looks as if you haven't bought your own idea, why should anyone else?

I have one simple rule if you're going to be out telling your story so that people will follow you:

If you're excited, notify your face!

Your face is your most important visual aid. Make sure you have natural intensity for your vision. You should—you helped dream it up. Now just show it, or people won't follow you.

There's a story about a TV newscaster interviewing the devil.

"What is the greatest weapon you use with people? Is it lies? Jealousy? Hate?"

"No! The most successful tool I use is *indifference.*"

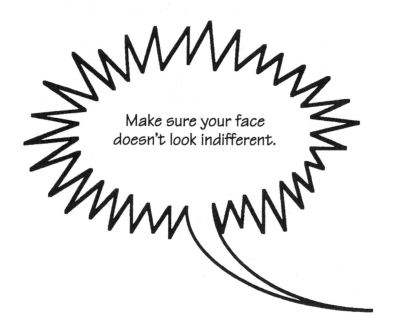

Make sure your face
doesn't look indifferent.

MAKE YOUR VISION A CAUSE

Most of us have noticed the zeal and fervor of people who work for nonprofit organizations. They are usually on fire about their cause.

Never was this brought home to me more clearly than when I participated in two annual symposia of the Windstar Foundation in Aspen, Colorado.

Eighteen hundred people gathered in the Aspen Music Festival tent for four days. Two-thirds of those attending worked for non-profit organizations. As the conference started tackling the hard issues of pollution, the people who worked for various nonprofits were downright passionate about their beliefs and what they were doing.

I instruct my profit-oriented clients to define a vision they think of as a *cause*!

A normal corporate financial goal does not come close to igniting the same natural energy that can burn inside you when you have a cause.

A cause makes you catch on fire.

So,

Most people need to lead through their voice, not their position. When you have a vision that you now see as a *cause*, your voice is naturally more passionate. It changes its pace and tone. You sound excited. And you look excited.

What's happening is that you're looking and sounding *committed*. And until you do, no one else will follow you.

> Make your vision a cause!

> A vision that is a cause allows you to be naturally committed.

> Enthusiasm is catching.

> Passion is infectious.

As a presentation skills trainer, I know you need to have two ingredients going for you when you are talking to others, trying to get them to follow you:

1. Clarity

2. Caring

Clarity:

- When you have developed a crystal-clear vision and position, you should naturally be clear.

- Clarity allows for focused energy when you speak.

- Clarity allows you to be remembered so that you can be evaluated.

Caring:

- Since you created the vision and position based on discovering "what's important around here?" you've *platformed* your thinking on mutual values.

- Mutual values led to a mutual vision and position.

- This will naturally allow you to speak about the emotional benefits of a *joint* vision.

- You will demonstrate natural caring to your listeners. They will like you. They will trust you. They will follow you.

Great leaders are committed to their vision. It becomes their cause.

To summarize,

- A good vision makes you passionately compelled to make it happen.

- Leaders are shamelessly enthusiastic about their vision.

- Laser clarity communicates that you care and you demonstrate natural commitment.

- People don't care how much you know until they know how much you care.

Make your vision a cause. When you talk, you'll be *naturally* committed. People will follow you.

So—Learn to Motivate

CHAPTER CHECKLIST

✔ Being good on your feet is a *must.* It isn't enough just to be competent; you need to be able to communicate your competence or you're not effective.

✔ Sell the *benefits* of the vision, especially the emotional benefits.

✔ You need to discover what your people could have a vested interest in. Then it's much easier to motivate them—in fact, this is the *only* way to motivate them.

✔ It's mandatory to motivate others so that they help you get to the promised land. Plus, it's a lot more fun to work in a place where the energy ambiance is high.

✔ Getting people excited so that they act in a focused direction is the trick—not just getting them excited.

✔ Telling your story *a lot* is the territory of the leader.

✔ Skills are needed so that you don't appear to be on your deathbed while presenting. How you *look* and *sound* actually does more to establish trust and believability in listeners than the words you speak. One way to have a quick check is to make sure you notify your face if you're excited.

Think of your credo as a cause. It will make you naturally more intense. More committed. More clear. More caring.

Conclusion

NOW WHAT DO I DO?

That's All Very Interesting —What's Next?

Peters and Waterman, in their book *In Search of Excellence*, feel that one trait excellent companies have in common is their propensity to act—the "ready, fire, aim" concept.

Nike tennis shoe ads shout at us to "Just Do It!"

As promised, I've tried to say simply what you need to do and talk about so that people follow you. Also, you must spend a good deal of your time communicating, telling your story, and getting skilled at telling your story.

I've tried to follow Albert Einstein's rule: "If you can't say it simply, you probably don't have anything to say. And if you can't say it simply, you don't know your subject."

So I've listed twenty steps to go do, steps that will help you become a skilled motivator.

I urge you to act. To lead. To make a difference. To discover for yourself and others where you all really want to go, what kind of place you want to work in, and the cause about which you can all get excited.

TWENTY STEPS TO DO

THE TWENTY STEPS

1. Discover your own values. What's important to you?

2. Discover what direction lights a fire under you. What can become a *cause?*

3. Define what you believe to be the benefits to each of your key players, the people you want to have following you.

4. Discover what *their* key values are. What's important around here?

5. Hold a Vision Quest. Discover where your people want to go, what turns them on.

6. Define a mutual vision based on shared values.

7. Develop a list of logical and emotional benefits that make the vision a salable product to *all* your people.

8. Present the mutual vision and its benefits to your key people. Get agreement. Now you have the

- Mutual vision

- Shared values it's based on

- Benefits for all to become committed to it

9. Create Camp Credo with key people.

- Define who you'll be to attain your vision.

- Define your credo.

- Flesh out the strategies and tactics to execute the plan to attain the vision.

- Agree on the plan.

10. Realize that risk has become part of your vision and plan. Risk will seem natural because it's taken in the context of

- Mutual vision

- Shared values

- Shared benefits

11. Create the tools needed to go into the market to execute the plan. Get serious. Begin to act.

12. Hold a Vision Day for all your people. Sell them

    - What's important around here

    - The vision

    - Your company credo, and why it will institutionalize your vision

    - The benefits to everyone from committing energy and skill to the plan and vision

13. *Demand* loyalty to

    - The values

    - The vision

    - The credo

14. Weed out the nonbelievers. They are neither wrong nor dumb if they don't agree with you. They're just on the wrong ship going in the wrong direction.

15. Create a sales capability presentation that supports your credo.

16. Practice the principle of concentration for *all* resources to back your credo. Concentration is the secret to all economic success.

17. Reward risk taking to attain the vision. Don't just expect risk, *reward* risk.

18. Turn the credo into a *cause by* repeated communication to all levels. Do it in person. Get out of your office. Be *the* chief salesperson for the vision and credo.

19. Celebrate measurable success. Celebrate measurable effort.

20. Once the vision is close to becoming a reality, create a new one. People want challenges that benefit their lives. Recreate—refocus—redefine a new direction based on the same shared values.

ONE LAST PERSONAL NOTE

My father was in a nursing home for four years before he died. He had Alzheimer's disease—a progressive degeneration of the brain. It took a while to figure out what to do when I visited him. He wouldn't greet me. Usually he said nothing—just sat with his head hanging. It was hard to know if he was comprehending anything I said.

On one visit, I pulled out my calendar and started talking about my upcoming schedule. His head remained hanging as I went over plans, hopes, and dreams. Then the moment happened that has remained my directive. He lifted his head and said the only words he'd said in weeks: "Then get on with it, Son!"

About the Author

Bob Boylan is a Leadership and Presentation Coach for middle and senior management. His style and techniques are singularly focused on **Delivering Training That Takes.**

This book is an example of his trademark . . . to deliver *easily understood, memorable,* and *realistically actionable* principles and techniques. These are ideas that "take" . . . so you lead more effectively!

Bob resides 50/50 between his two residences in Minneapolis and Aspen.

For more information, contact:

Successful Presentations
A Division of Boylan Enterprises, Inc.
3195 Casco Circle, Minneapolis, MN 5391
612/471-8917 (telephone)
612/471-8928 (fax)
1-800-944-7048